Marketing Plan Template

Writing Marketing Plans for Small Business

Chris Gattis and Felica Sparks

www.BusinessStartup101.com

Marketing Plan Template

Chris Gattis and Felica Sparks

www.BusinessStartup101.com

For information on discounts for bulk purchases and our other products, please contact Blue Point Publishers at books@bluepointstrategies.com.

ISBN-13: 978-1468019728
ISBN-10: 1468019724

Printed in The United States of America

Contents

Introduction

The marketing plan brings together all the market research, product discussion, customer pondering, and calculating that you've done and uses that information to promote your business brand and your products and services in such a way that your target customers know about your business offerings and are compelled to buy your products and services. If you bring all these pieces together correctly and follow up by delivering products and services that exceed your customers' expectations, you will build a loyal following that will reward you with a successful and growing business.

For most small businesses and start-ups, marketing is some sort of "black magic" that isn't really understood. Most hopeful entrepreneurs that I coach think they don't understand marketing at all. I'm not suggesting that developing a creative marketing plan is simple. But it's more about doing your research and laying out a logical plan based on that research than it is "black magic" wizardry.

Keep in mind that you'll develop a separate plan for each market segment. You'll need to approach each segment and target customer with a unique strategy. While some or possibly all parts will be the same, you should assume that all parts will be different for each market segment. After you get all the pieces laid out, you can combine and overlap where it makes sense to take best advantage of your available budget.

We like to approach developing a marketing plan just like developing a business plan. Do your market research first, then develop strategies based on customers and preferences, consider the financial implications, and launch. Use the template; adopt the steps to your business, products and market; develop the strategy and action plans; and put your plan into action. The businesses are different, the products are different, the people are different, but the steps required to develop the plan are essentially the same. This plan has been developed to make it as easy as possible to develop a creative and effective plan for marketing your business and products. It's been used over and over in our firm as we work with clients from different industries. We start every job the same way; at the beginning of the template doing our research.

A few definitions may be in order before reading further. The following terms are used in this book to describe markets, functions, and tools used in the marketing area.

Market Analysis: This is a brief restatement of the market conditions, trends, and major opportunities and threats.

Market Segments: Market segments define the different subgroups within an industry. For example, within the legal industry, there are market segments for corporate law, elder law, criminal defense, personal injury, and so forth. In many cases, each of these segments will also have sub segments. As a marketer, you will be looking to certain segments and sub segments in which to do business. You will not do business in every segment in your industry. You will be developing a specific marketing plan for each of these target segments, or markets.

Target Customer: Target customers are your most likely customers. It's a group of potential customers with similar interests, needs, likes, or demographic makeup. These are the people or businesses that you think will most likely want your services. The needs and wants of this group are what you will build your marketing plan around.

Unique Sales Proposition: This is sometimes called a unique value proposition. Why would your target customer hire you instead of the firm down the street offering the same service? It's a statement or idea that sets you apart from your competition. In other words, what makes your firm so special? Remember, it's all about the customer.

Marketing Strategy: Your marketing strategy is a plan that will be defined in terms of the 4 P's of marketing: product, price, place, and promotion.

Product: Your 'product' may be either a physical product or a service. What products or services will you promote to your target customer and how will the customer use them? How does your service solve the target customer's problem or make their life better? These questions will help you define your product or service offering to your target customer. You will concentrate your offering based on the wants and needs of your target customer.

Price: Will you price higher or lower than your competition? What are the advantages of your pricing strategy relative to your brand and service level? Include list price, discounts, payment terms, and any other financial terms, such as leasing or financing options. This category usually seems obvious, but you need to make a conscious decision to price in a particular way.

Place: How will you get your product or service to the customer? The distribution channel you use will have a major impact on the pricing and promotion of the service. Will you use one channel exclusively (i.e. retail, direct, distribution, or manufacturer's rep) or some combination? The model you use may largely depend on your industry. Especially if you have a small firm, you may not be able to change how business is already being done in your industry. In any case, you want to use the channel or channels that work best for your target customer.

Promotion: The promotion plan will be defined by outlining your goals or market objectives, budget, timetable, and resources necessary to implement the promotion of your services and your firm.

Goals (Market Objectives): Goals can be defined as selling a certain dollar amount or number of services or commanding a certain percentage of the total market. In some cases, you'll be trying to raise awareness of your firm and your capabilities. In these cases, you will not have a hard dollar or percentage increase but an awareness increase. Be careful of this type of goal because it is very difficult to measure.

Budget: The budget is the amount of money set aside for individual pieces of the marketing plan or the plan as a whole. Don't forget to include any R&D that might be necessary to get a service ready for market, administrative support necessary to implement the plan and any other costs associated with the promotion launch.

Timetable: The timetable is the amount of time needed to accomplish the goals of your marketing plan or individual tactic. This includes time necessary to develop any marketing materials or websites in addition to the time needed to launch and run the actual tactic.

Resources: What resources are necessary to meet your goals? You have already defined the cash requirement for the tactic, but what about employees, research costs, accounting, graphic art, web page, and other expenses?

Action Plan/Implementation Tactics: What, specifically, are you going to do to promote your business or products? You'll be defining the specific implementation tactics necessary to promote your services including the action items and scheduling. This is what most people think of as marketing. In reality, it's one of the end results of all your planning and research efforts.

Advertising and Promotion: How will you advertise your products or services? Will you use media, such as TV, radio, newspapers, magazines, trade journals, and billboards? Or will you use Internet marketing, e-mail campaigns, pay-per-click advertising, or social media?

PR Campaigns: PR campaigns include news conferences, YouTube videos, press releases, and industry website news to promote your services and/or company launch? There are many different definitions of advertising and PR. For our purposes here, we'll use this simple definition: advertising is bought; PR is free.

Networking: Networking can take the form of chamber of commerce "after hours" or breakfast events or a more formal networking such as Business Networking International (BNI). While many of these options do not have a direct cost, they do take time, something which may be in shorter supply than actual cash money.

Monitor/Measure/Test: One of the most important pieces of your marketing plan is the measurement. If you have set goals and objectives for your plans, you'll be able to measure the results. If you aren't getting the results you wanted, make changes to your plan. Describe how you will monitor the plans and measure your results.

Research Tools

In order to identify and understand your market, segments, competition, distribution channels, and customers, you're going to have to do some research. Even a seasoned industry pro will start by doing research. Where will you get the information that you need? There are many sources of information and in the age of the Internet, maybe in some cases, too many sources. Be careful where your research-produced information comes from. There are as many "experts" on the Internet as there are websites with content. Just because someone wrote a blog entry about your profession does not mean that the information is factual or that the blogger is an expert. Anyone can create a website and pretend to be an expert. Some do this as a means of promoting a political position or a personal economic incentive. Keep in mind where your "data" comes from and make sure it's a source that you trust.

Here is a listing of a few common sources of market, customer, and company information:

Census Bureau: The Census Bureau has some excellent demographic information available from their website, http://factfinder2.census.gov/. This information is free to the public and is available from any computer with an Internet connection. You can sort the information by state, county, city, zip code, school district, and many other categories. You can get valuable information about your potential customers based on their income, age, educational attainment, type of work, and so forth. You can really only understand the vast amount of alternatives available by visiting the site and familiarizing yourself with the many options.

Public Library: The local public library has many sources of market data. Many larger libraries have extensive periodicals, from multifamily apartment construction to zoo management. Look through the magazines and journals to see whether they have subscriptions to ones that might be interesting to your particular profession or industry. They might have many years of old periodicals and newspapers on file. In addition, they will likely have technical and financial books relating to companies and industries that you can view in the reference section.

Many large libraries have a reference librarian whose job it is to help you find information that you need. If you are pleasant and courteous, they will normally bend over backwards to assist you in your search for information. If you explain that you are developing a marketing plan and trying to find some information about an industry, segment, or competitor, the reference librarian will give you some possible sources and might even do some searching for you.

Library cards are generally available for free to members of the community. If you live out of town, you might have to pay a small fee for a library card, which gives you the privilege to check out materials and use the library's on-line resources. Many libraries have subscriptions to on-line commercial databases that make your research easier and more convenient. You can generally access these resources through the library website from the comfort of your home or office.

Virtual Library: Virtual library cards are available for using the many sources of nonpublic information. These sources could be public policy institutes, research, or databases maintained by universities, public or private companies, and other research related sites. The information is generally only available to educational or research organizations and requires a special subscription. Many public libraries have these subscriptions and make them available to their patrons. This virtual library card can usually be used from your home computer by logging into the library's information portal. Just ask the library employees whether your local library offers a virtual library card.

University Library: Just like the public libraries, most university libraries are open for use by the local community. If you aren't sure, give them a call. For serious research about specific topics, university librarians are generally happy to assist. They're used to working with students and will gladly help business persons who approach them with a friendly attitude and gracious spirit.

Chamber of Commerce: Many local chambers of commerce have subscriptions to databases of census and geographic information services (GIS) that can be made available to their members. Many large chambers have staff available to assist in research for new company recruitment and member business expansion and large projects. If you are unsure, call your chamber and ask whether they can help.

Small Business Administration: The SBA has lots of resources for hopeful and existing entrepreneurs alike. Just visit the website www.sba.gov.

Paid Sources: For larger companies or big marketing campaigns, there are many different sources of paid industry content. Sources such as Hoover's, Dunn & Bradstreet, IBISWorld, Demographics Now, and others offer industry specific information on the competitive landscape, demographics, trends, industry size, and critical issues that are updated on a regular basis. This information is available on a paid subscription basis. In addition, census data merged with consumer buying patterns and preferences are now available from several different companies. This information is relatively expensive, but it is used to be available only to the largest retail giants and consulting firms that can afford programming staff to generate the data. Many public or university libraries now offer limited access to this type data through their subscriptions. For large campaigns with high risk factors, this type data may be worth whatever the price.

Trade Associations: Most industries have one or more trade associations that serve as advocates for the industry. In many large industries, there may be several different groups serving similar needs for different segments of the industry. You may have to join the association to access their data, but they typically are an excellent source of specific and relevant information about your industry. If you don't find what you're looking for on their website, call the office and speak with a representative. Again, these individuals are generally more than willing to assist a potential new member to find the information that they are seeking.

Market Testing: If you need specific information about consumer buying habits, you probably need to do some market testing. Most people over the age of forty remember the Coke vs. Pepsi taste tests on TV. This 'market testing' was actually a Pepsi commercial, but the idea behind the commercial was a valid market test for consumers taste preference in soft drinks. One upscale clothing chain conducted a nearly year-long market test to see how the color of their sales staff's suits affected the purchasing habits of their customers. Most companies will not need this extensive preference testing, but if your potential service rollout is very large and costly, it might make sense to acquire some reliable consumer preference information before launching into a full-blown advertising campaign. You can do this with focus groups, service testing, surveys, and interviews, among others. This type of research can be done by the owner, but unless you truly understand how this process works or have the time to research and study how to do it, it's better left to professionals. While this may be the most expensive type of market research you conduct, it may also be the most helpful.

Focus Groups: Focus groups are an important component of market research. This type of research can be conducted on a formal or informal basis. The type of study you use will depend on how much money you have budgeted and the size of the firm's launch of services. An informal focus group might include a one-on-one discussion with customers, employees, service vendors and firm management to gather information about your company and market perceptions. If your risk is high or you need exacting information about style or substance relating to branding or service presentation, you might need to conduct formal focus groups. A semi-scientific method might be selecting individuals from a group of customers, service vendors, employees, and friends who meet specific demographic characteristics. It can give you a quick and inexpensive group on which to test your ideas. If the stakes or the risks are really high, you will probably want to hire a professional firm to conduct the group studies. If you don't know how to do this, get some help.

You should conduct some market behavior research as a part of your everyday business information gathering. How does the way your employees are dressed affect customer behavior? What about how you greet your customers on the phone or in person? To be effective, you must measure what you're doing and the results you get. The only way to get valuable information is to make changes to your system and measure the results compared to the results you got before the change. You may need to try several iterations before you hit on the best method or style. Data gathering in every part of your business is the only way to truly measure the variables in place and the results that were produced.

The Marketing Plan Template

This book will be laid out in sections. We'll give you the template first with details and explanation following. If you understand the template, you can whiz right through the process. If there's something you need a little help with, read the details.

The Marketing Plan Template is comprised of three main steps: research, strategy, and tactics. All good marketing plans begin with research. The second step is developing a strategy followed by tactics or action plan. Finally, while not a regular step in developing the process, you need to monitor the results from your marketing plan to ensure that you get the exposure, sales, or other benefits you planned for in your strategy.

The Marketing Plan Template

Market Research
Industry
Competition
Customers
Company

Marketing Strategy
Unique Sales Proposition
Brand
Product or Service
Promotion Goals

Action Plans
Advertising & Promotion
PR Campaigns
Networking
Putting it to Work

Monitor

This template system will allow you to break down your marketing plan activity into four steps: 1) market research, 2) marketing strategy, 3) promotion tactics, and 4) metrics. In the first step, you will conduct research on the industry, competition, customers, and your company. This is an important step not to be skipped. Step 2 involves determining how you will set your company apart from your competition, what your goals are, and how you'll do business based on the research you completed in Step 1. Step 3 involves developing action plans that will put your marketing goals into practice. This is where you'll buy advertising, network, and conduct social media marketing efforts, depending on what makes sense for your business. Step 4 involves comparing the results derived from the previous steps to your goals and making the necessary changes to your plan to maximize your results. You'll want to constantly tweak your plans to bring a continuous improvement philosophy to your marketing plan.

The actual action plans that you put into place will depend on your research and how you want to communicate with your target customers. The specific action plans, or tactics, will be different for every firm and service line. This is where you get to use your creativity to communicate your company values to the marketplace.

In the next three chapters, we'll outline and describe the first three steps involved in creating a marketing plan. Then we'll look at specific tactics for attorneys followed by a brief discussion of metrics. If you jump ahead to The Action Plan, don't forget to come back and work through the first steps. Starting at the end will result in a thrown together plan that doesn't address the concerns of your target customers and will most likely be ineffective.

Market Research

The first part of your plan, as we've said before, is the research portion. You'll want to break down your research into four categories: 1) industry & markets, 2) competition, 3) customers, and 4) company. The market analysis template is as follows.

Market Research

Industry
    Description of Industry
    Industry Trends
    Market Segment(s)
    Distribution Channels

Competition
    Direct & Indirect Competition
    Strengths & Weaknesses

Customers
    Demographics

Company
>   Company Profile
>
>   SWOT Analysis

Industry

Understanding your market is one of the important first steps in preparing to develop a marketing plan. Understanding how your market works, the size and potential for either a new company, or an expanded role for an existing company in the market structure is each a key component. Who are your competitors and why would a potential customer buy from you? Understanding the market is the most important part of the marketing process.

While this part seems to be simple and is often overlooked or skipped, it requires a serious analysis of each component. Brainstorm and research each market segment in which you will compete, and then boil down the results into a form to help you "see" the market at a glance. Once you've assembled all the information, list it in a matrix format to get an "at a glance" view of your market. You may also use the Market Matrix Worksheet that is available for download at www.BusinessStartup101.com.

Some of the critical questions you need to answer are:

How big is the market?

In actual dollar sales, how much combined do all the participants in the market sell? Can the market support another competitor? Knowing how big the market is and who has the major share will help you determine your strategy.

What percent of the market share do you want or need?

Based on your own financial projections, what percentage share of the market do your sales represent? Is that a reasonable percentage? If the financial projections show your company with a large percentage of the market share, do a reality check with your advisors or mentors to confirm your projections and assumptions.

If you are hoping to be a national market player, how will the large competitors in the market react to your entry into the market and subsequent rise from a small company that they can ignore to a real competitor?

What are the different market segments?

Most industries have many different segments that make up a market. For example, in the hand tools market, there are segments for woodworking, vehicle repair, machinery repair, and many specialty segments. Within each segment, there are sub-segments. For example, within the woodworking segment, there are sub-segments for the casual home repair novice or apartment dweller, the weekend handyman doing major home repairs and remodeling, and the professional tradesmen. Almost all industries have several to dozens of market segments and hundreds of sub and sub-sub segments.

In what market segment will your company compete?

Known as your target market, this is the primary market segment in which you will compete. If you manufacture specialty hand tools for professional commercial HVAC installation and repair, you will not be as concerned about the casual home repair novice or apartment dweller market. It is important to identify in which specific market segment or segments you will compete and learn as much about how those segments work as possible.

Many markets likely already have a dominant player who serves a broad section of the market, perhaps operating across many different segments. How will you compete with this dominant player? Perhaps you can find a niche segment or sub-segment in which to operate. If you're not looking to awaken the sleeping giant, the major player in the market, perhaps your best bet is to think small. By that, I mean to operate within a small niche at first to prove your model and fine-tune your business skills. After you have smoothed out the rough spots in your operating model or product offering, only then might you want to expand your business to serve a larger segment.

Distribution Channels

Distribution channels are the way in which you'll get your products or services to your customers. How you go to market can be largely defined by your individual market. If everyone in the market uses the same distribution method and your target customer prefers that method, then you're probably limited to operating largely with that distribution method. That's not to say you can't offer your products or services through other channels, but be prepared to be underwhelmed by the response from your customers. However, business is an ever changing dynamic, and new models are designed and tested every day. Who's to say your new distribution channel isn't the next best method? Do your research, know your customer preferences, and test your methods before investing lots of money in an untested method. Who would have guessed in 1990 that movies would be rented by downloading them directly from your TV and not by driving to a retail store where you would browse the shelves in search of your favorite film in VHS format?

What is your distribution strategy? What channels will you use? How do the standard distribution channels affect the way you plan to do business? Do you need partnerships with distributors, sales reps, manufacturer's reps, or other resellers? Understand the standard channels in your market, how you'll do business the same or differently, and what you can do to differentiate yourself from the competition. How can you improve the standard channel models to make it easier for your customers to do business with you versus your competition?

If you are a reseller, do you have the support of a manufacturer? Don't make the mistake of thinking that any manufacturer will sell you product. Manufacturers who use a distributor channel model may already have distributors for each of the markets they serve. If you plan to enter a mature market, you may have some difficulty getting the support from a manufacturer.

Competition

Determine who your direct and indirect competitors are in the target market you will serve. What's the difference between "direct" and "indirect" competition? Direct competitors offer the same type products as you and operate a similar business in the same market. If you own a local diner serving breakfast and lunch to locals, your direct competition would be other small, quick-service restaurants, fast-food establishments, and maybe coffee shops and convenience stores. They all offer a quick meal at a low or reasonable price. Your indirect competitors are grocery stores, fine dining establishments, and national companies that deliver food frozen or specially packaged foods via mail or delivery service. These type companies all provide food, but it's not a quick, inexpensive breakfast or lunch meal.

Make a list of the direct competition within your geographic market. Understand how they do business, the types of products or services in which they specialize, and to the best of your ability, their strengths and weaknesses. That is, what do they do well and not so well?

I find it helpful, especially in markets where the location of the company is an important factor in the consumers' decision to buy or not buy, to mark each competitor's location on a map.

This specific location reference can help you identify strengths and weaknesses that are geographical in nature and that might not be obvious at first. Pay attention to traffic counts and demographic patterns in the market.

Also make a list of your indirect competitors. Their presence and obvious strengths and weaknesses will help you identify niches in the market and develop strategies to leverage your strengths or your competitor's weaknesses.

Don't think for a moment that you don't have any competition. It's not true. You have competition. Even if there is a brand new market emerging, someone else can mobilize in reaction to it with more people and more money than you. That you've poured your heart and soul and maybe life savings into this venture is irrelevant. Your competition is in the business to make money, and you now represent a threat to them.

How will you differentiate yourself and your business from every other business in your market segment? This question is at the heart of your business model, your product or service offering, and your distribution channel. How will you do business better, smarter, cheaper, faster, or more responsively to customer needs than your competition? Be careful of going for the cheaper angle. Your biggest competitors probably have much better cost models than you and could easily destroy you in a price war. Customers don't always respond to the cheapest price model in the ways you would expect. You have to carefully consider your market segment, what your competition is doing, how they price and go to market, and then find your niche in an underserved segment.

Can you make money in this business? After looking at your direct and indirect competitors, now is a good time to look at their pricing compared to your pricing. How does your cost to produce the product or service relate to the prices your competition charges? What are the advantages and disadvantages of pricing higher or lower than your competition?

For a small business, it is highly unlikely that you will be able to move the market to your costs. Unless you've discovered a way to make the product or service at significantly reduced costs, you should probably assume that you'll have to charge a price similar to that of your competition. If you think you can produce the product at a significantly reduced price, you should go back and confirm your numbers. Ask yourself, what's different about the way we will make the product and go to market that allows us to do it a reduced cost? Make sure you understand all the costs involved in going to market. Many large companies have whole teams of engineers and accountants studying cost reduction and best practices in manufacturing so that they can tweak another penny or nickel out of their costs. You don't have that kind of team and couldn't hope to buy in the quantities of your biggest competitors, except in rare circumstances.

Is it really an advantage to be the cheapest seller in the market? For many consumer products, Wal-Mart has been the price leader. And against their revenues in the hundreds of billions of dollars through 8,000+ retail outlets, you'll never be able to compete with them on price. And do you really want to try? Having the lowest price may work against you, depending on your market. If you are selling consumer products, then you'll need to be at least competitive with your pricing. But if you're selling high-tech scientific services, low prices may give your target customers the feeling that you aren't very good at what you do. The point is the price you charge for your products or services should be part of your strategy. Which market segments you serve, which customers you target, the specific product or service you offer, how you go to market, and what prices you charge are all part of your model and should be thought about carefully with the end result of serving your target customers in mind. Don't pick any of those strategies haphazardly.

Customers

Who are your customers? Do you sell to individuals or other businesses? Try to break down your customer base into logical categories. If you sell to consumers, use demographic categories. The more precisely you can identify your customer base, whether individuals or other businesses, the more efficiently you can promote your business.

If you do business with individuals, business-to-consumer (B2C), then identify the demographic categories that best describe your customer. Use any demographic category that makes sense for your business, such as age, sex, marital status, income, or education. There are many additional categories like home ownership, religious preference, school affiliation, and so forth. Use those categories that make sense for your product line and market.

In addition, identify where your customers live, work, play, eat, worship, what kind of vehicle they drive, and anything else that is identifiable. We find that many times small businesses don't really understand their customer. What about their income, age, or behavior makes them interesting to you? What about your product, service, mission, or corporate philosophy makes you interesting to your potential customer?

Likewise, if you do business with other companies, business-to-business (B2B), try to identify those characteristics that make your customer base identifiable. The more clearly you can identify your customer, the more accurate you can be when defining your marketing strategy.

Clearly define your target customer in the appropriate categories. Depending on your business, you may have defined an even more precise measurement system. If you have actual historical data from this or another business that closely matches yours, use that information to get a better feel for your customer and their behaviors.

Company

Just as you looked closely at your competition to identify what they do well and not so well, you need to now turn the magnifying glass inward. Take a critical look at your own company and how you operate in your market. One way we do this is with a tool called a SWOT analysis.

SWOT Analysis

At this point in the process, you should have a good idea of the trends in your industry and within your specific market segment, as well as what your competitors do well and not so well. Additionally, you should understand what your customers need, want, and desire. We'll now pull all this information together in the form of a SWOT analysis. SWOT stands for Strengths, Weaknesses, Opportunities and Threats. The SWOT analysis is at the heart of the marketing process and will help you identify where opportunities in the market match the strengths of your company. These intersections are sweet-spots for you where your company can take advantage of market opportunities with existing capital, employee knowledge, or technology. It will also help identify where threats and weaknesses cross so you can make strategic plans to improve your company performance in these areas.

Management theory typically breaks down the SWOT into internal and external environments, where strengths and weaknesses are internal to the firm and where opportunities and threats are external to the market factors. While this breakdown makes sense in many instances, it can sometimes be confusing. (Are the strengths and weaknesses of your competition opportunities or threats?) What is important to understand is that the SWOT analysis will help you identify your resources and capabilities and how they match up against the other players in your market. It will identify what your firm is prepared to do better than your competition and what your customers expect that your operation is ill prepared to provide.

The SWOT analysis begins to help you differentiate your company from your competition and to help you successfully compete in a tough market.

Strengths

What are your organization's strengths?

Your strengths should be measured relative to your competition and the expectations of your customers. Following this internal-external theme, strengths are an internal analysis of how your company is prepared to compete in the market. A few examples of strengths are:

Technology: Strengths in technology might include patents, proprietary manufacturing methods, special equipment, production capacity, IT systems, or special software.

Manufacturing: Manufacturing strengths might include manufacturing systems with a significant cost advantage or supply partnerships not available to other market participants.

Financial: Financial strengths might include a large cash reserve or untapped borrowing capability, low borrowing costs, or available investor base.

Geographic: Geographic strengths might include being ideally located in regard to suppliers, fabricators, or customers.

Employees: Perhaps your company has a solid base of experienced and dedicated employees who provide excellent service to your customer base.

Strengths can come in many different forms, whether people, technology, brand, financial resources, or even strong customer loyalty.

Weaknesses

Like strengths, your weaknesses should be measured relative to your competition and customer expectations. In some cases, a weakness is the flip side of a strength. While an experienced staff may be a strength in providing customer support, it's also expensive to have a large and experienced staff. Also, having plenty of production capacity may be a strength, but it's also a weakness in that your machines aren't running constantly throughout the day. Like strengths, the weaknesses analysis is a look inside your organization and how it's prepared to compete in the marketplace. Some examples of weaknesses are:

Technology: Technology weaknesses might include old customer management software that doesn't give you adequate capabilities, internal systems that aren't integrated, or systems with glitches.

Manufacturing: Manufacturing weaknesses include lack of production capacity, outdated equipment with high operating and maintenance costs, inability to buy supplies at the best rates, and lack of physical space.

Brand: Brand weaknesses include poor or no reputation in the market and a strong connection with a former product line as you switch direction.

Financial: High cost of money, tapped out borrowing lines, no investors on hand, and high existing debt burden are examples of financial weaknesses.

Employees: Employee weaknesses include low employee morale, new and untrained employees in a high technology or complicated product line, and high absenteeism.

It's important to make an honest assessment of your position within the market. Kidding yourself will result in money spent on advertising and promotional efforts to the wrong market, wrong customers, or with the wrong product. These aforementioned categories are merely examples of possible weaknesses. Use any category or theme that is appropriate for your company.

Opportunities

What are your organization's opportunities?

With the opportunities analysis, we get to look outside the company at the market environment. How is your competition responding to the customer's needs? What niches are left unfilled or what product lines unproduced or poorly serviced? Examples of opportunities are:

Legal/Regulatory: Opportunities in the legal and regulatory area include new environmental regulations with which your company is already compliant, new IRS rules that your accounting software is already configured to meet, or packaging or labeling requirements with which your company already complies.

Competition: Competition opportunities might include a major competitor exiting the market, consolidation within the market, or an emerging market in which no competition has yet to emerge.

Vertical Market: Perhaps a new vertical market develops where your company already has capabilities and production capacity.

Technology: New technology opportunities might exist from expansion of existing equipment or patents owned by your company.

Market Research

Contracts: Opportunities in demand might occur from major new contract appropriations, seasonal product demand, or trade barrier removal.

Threats

What are your organization's threats?

Like opportunities, threats come from the market, or external environment. Examples of threats are:

Political: Political or legislative changes in your industry might cause significant compliance issues.

Technology: Technology threats might include the requirement to utilize a new expensive technology to comply with environmental requirements or possibly just an upgrade to your existing IT systems that will cause outages to service.

Substitution: Substitute products, like a generic in the pharmaceutical world, might put significant manufacturing cost pressures on your sales efforts.

Trends: Industry trends, like those facing the movie rental business, might force you to significantly change how you do business.

Changes to the external environment may provide opportunities to some and present threats to others. Depending on your own strengths and weaknesses, your company may view these market changes differently than does your competition. Remember, these are just a few examples of the types of categories of strengths, weaknesses, opportunities, and threats your company may face. Conduct brainstorming sessions with your leadership team to compare your company to the market in which you operate, the competition, and the needs and wants of your customer base.

Analysis

It may be helpful to arrange the four categories in a simple grid. Draw a vertical and horizontal line across and through the middle of a sheet a paper or white board. Think of the left hand side of the grid as the internal environment, or your company. Think of the right hand side of the grid as the external environment, or your market. The top left box is the strengths with the weaknesses on the bottom left. Opportunities are placed in the top right box with threats in the bottom right box.

As you study the top half of the box, you can compare your strengths with the opportunities in the market. Which strengths give you a natural advantage with which opportunities? Are any of the opportunities natural fits with your strengths?

Likewise, as you look at the threats in the marketplace, are there weaknesses that can be corrected to allow you to better leverage your company to fight? Maybe you were thinking of a new product line that now has significant threats because of industry trends that are just now being exposed by your research.

The SWOT analysis is a two part exercise. Not only do you have to identify the items for the four categories, but then you analyze how to move forward based on this information. Where will you place operating priorities based on the competition, market forces, and your company's ability to compete? This tool is a useful framework for making important strategic decisions about your direction and priorities.

SWOT Analysis Grid

Internal Environment	External Environment
Strengths	Opportunities
Weaknesses	Threats

As you study the top half of the box, you can compare your strengths with the opportunities in the market. Which strengths give you a natural advantage with which opportunities? Are any of the opportunities natural fits with your strengths?

Likewise, as you look at the threats in the marketplace, are there weaknesses that can be corrected to allow you to better leverage your company to fight? Maybe you were thinking of a new service line that now has significant threats because of industry trends that are just now being exposed by your research.

The SWOT analysis is a two-part exercise. Not only do you have to identify the items for the four categories, but then you must analyze how to move forward based on this information. Where will you place operating priorities based on the competition, market forces, and your firm's ability to compete? This tool is a useful framework for making important strategic decisions about your direction and priorities.

Marketing Strategy

You've done all your research and think you're ready to start selling your product. How do you know you've got the product or service right? Like every other step in this process, you need a well-defined goal and plan to get you there. Outside of running out of cash, lacking a marketing plan is one of the leading causes of business failure. Having the right product, at the right price, in the right place, with the right promotion is a difficult balancing act.

Marketing Strategy
Unique Sales Proposition
Brand
Product or Service
Promotion Goals

Unique Sales Proposition

What makes your company so special? We touched on this idea earlier. If you don't know, how will your customers know? Hopefully, you have a very clear and organized way of thinking about how you are different from your competition. We call this your unique value proposition (UVP) or unique selling proposition (USP).

You probably decided to go into your particular line of business because you have a clearly defined USP. You hate the way your industry or old employer handles a particular situation, and you want a company that does it differently. Maybe it has to do with building customer loyalty or how you treat employees. Whatever your particular USP, you need to define it in a way that your customers can not only understand it, but also embrace it.

Let's face it; your customers do not care that you feel passionately about a particular cause or situation. They care only about what it means to them. If you feel strongly that you will use only recycled packaging and shipping materials, what does that mean for them? Unless it means you'll have a cheaper price, lower shipping costs, or can tie the recycling to some specific benefit to the environment or local market, they probably will not really care. If you haven't got a good answer to that, then you need to put your thinking cap on and figure it out. If you can't put into words how you are different and why your customers will care, then they probably will not care, and you probably are not different from your competition at all. Be honest with yourself, and don't try to fabricate something out of nothing.

Brand

What's your brand? We used to think of brand as a logo or group of stylized words and colors. Clever marketers even dream up fanciful words like ultra-surfactant quotient and X-43 Super Clean to push their brands. Since the beginning of time, clever marketers have been trying to come up with more and more fantastic adjectives to describe their products to make them seem more interesting. "BUY THOR'S WHEELS, CUT ROUND FOR A SMOOTHER RIDE!" Savvy consumers and businesses don't fall for code words or slick logos as a replacement for the values of the company.

Your brand should be an extension of who your company is, what it stands for, and how it does business. If that sounds like a tall order, it is. Creating the perfect marketing package takes more than just combining your products with cool logos to create a brand. And branding is way more than just fancy marketing. While the slick marketing piece will help play a role, it's the marriage of your brand message with the actions of the company that ultimately matter. In other words, reality must match your branding, or your customers will consider it all just more hype.

You have to first understand that all businesses are really providing a service. Whether your company is a "service" business or a manufacturer, distributor, retail, or wholesale, you are really providing a service. And what's worse, today's on-line virtual world has turned every competitor in the world into your competitor. The only real distinction comes down to service. It's not what you sell. It's how you sell it and how you support your customers after the purchase. How does your brand tell that story and does the brand story match the reality?

Mission/Vision Statement

A mission statement is a simple statement of what business you are in and why. This statement is the responsibility of the owners and senior management of a company to define and implement. Once written, the mission statement serves as the ground rules for operating the business. That is, each major decision of the company should somehow support the mission or vision of the organization. Small business owners ask if the mission statement isn't just some big company nonsense made up by Fortune 500 executives without a real job. I think the mission statement is just as important for small companies, maybe more important, than for their multinational counterparts. You should be able to use your mission statement to guide the company as you grow. If you are considering new ventures or product lines, they should first be measured against your mission statement to see if they support the overall goals of the organization. If not, you should reconsider the venture or your mission. All activities of your company should further your mission.

How can you succeed in a small business if you don't know what business you are in and why you are in that business? Without a clearly defined statement that you support and believe, you may wander aimlessly among your competitors, trying different courses and taking different paths without any real goal. Especially for a small business, your mission statement should be a defining document of your beliefs and objectives for going into business in the first place.

A mission statement can be a simple sentence or declaration, or a more complete summary of an organization's beliefs, values, and vision for its future. If you have a strong drive and vision for your company, here is your chance to share that belief and value system with your employees and customers.

For a mission or value statement to be effective in guiding your company direction and operations it should be a clearly stated and honestly held declaration of your beliefs, not some phony corporate speak. Your mission is a basic statement describing the overall purpose of your company. It is the first strategic decision the company should take. The mission should define your direction, priorities, and what sets you apart from your competitors. It should reflect the personality of the owners and help build the image of the organization. Ideally, it will motivate your employees and clarify the direction you will take on your path to success.

Whether your mission statement is long and involved or short and sweet, it must be real. Your customers and employees will be turned off by marketing hype that doesn't reflect the way you behave.

Product or Service

What is your product or service? You should be able to define your product in terms of what it does for the customer. How does it make the customer's life better, easier, faster or cheaper? How will your customer's life be improved by buying your product? What makes your product superior over every other similar product already on the market? If you can't think of a good answer to these questions, your customer probably can't either.

Describe, in detail, the products and services you will be selling. Your description should include a general description of each product or service, plus pricing models and distribution channels for each product or service.

Your company strengths and weaknesses will help you evaluate which opportunities are right for you and the threats to avoid. As you develop your products and service offering, keep in mind the needs, wants, and desires of your target customer. You might think that the latest add-on or upgrade to a do-dad is the hottest next thing in the market, but does your customer? Many a product or service has been designed and marketed only to find that no real market exists. While the company owner spent lots of money developing marketing plans and buying advertising, if there is no real market for a product or service, that money will have been wasted.

Talk to your customers, conduct focus groups or other market studies. Make sure that your prospective customers actually want to pay money for your particular product or service. One way is to select some individuals who are in your target customer group and ask them. If the difference in color, shape, size, and packaging is potentially important to the marketing effort, take the necessary time to understand these factors. If your plan is big and the risk is high, you might need to hire a market research firm to help determine which characteristics will be included in your product or service.

Make sure you understand the difference between features and benefits. A feature is a factual statement about a product or service; it's what products have. A benefit is what those features mean; it describes why your customer should care. Theodore Levitt, a 19th-century economist and Harvard University professor, described the difference like this: "People don't want to buy a quarter-inch drill; they want a quarter-inch hole."

Your customers care only about benefits. They are 'What's in it for me?' kind of people. In fact, everyone is a 'What's in it for me?' kind of person. As a manufacturer, you care about your product features; it has a little handle here, this one is blue, that button makes it fly higher, those straps keep it from falling off. As consumers, your customers only care about your product benefits; it's easy to carry, it matches my carpet,

I can feel the exhilaration, it's safe. Just keep in mind that you and your salespeople care only about features. Your customers care only about benefits.

Pricing

What will you charge for your product? Why? Will you have different pricing models for a retail environment versus a wholesale environment? How does your price compare to that of your competitors? How does your price compare to your cost of production? What are the benefits of being cheaper than your competitors? Are there benefits to being more expensive? How will you use payment terms and customer accounts to support your sales and financial goals?

Don't forget to think about total cost of product ownership. If the cost of your product doesn't end with the initial purchase, your customer will certainly be considering the total cost of ownership. If your sales price is cheap but operating the product is very expensive, your customer could become dissatisfied. Think about how your price compares to the cost of owning your product.

Distribution Channels

We discussed distribution channels at length during the research section. You should understand how your industry and target market segment(s) operate. How will you get your products and services into the hands of your customers? Will you utilize your own sales force or rely on manufacturer's reps or distributors? Analyze your choices and make a decision that best serves you and your customers.

Where will you sell your product? How will you go to market? Will you sell directly to the public through a retail environment, on-line to wholesalers, or something else? Will this be a catalog or direct mail type environment?

Promotion Goals

Marketing plans don't have to be complicated, but they do need to be well thought out. Identifying where you want to be or what outcome you hope to see from your efforts will help you lay out specific action plans to achieve the success you desire.

Identify the Goals

What do you want the marketing plan to accomplish? How long will it take? You need to establish specific market objectives and time frames for accomplishing your goals. If you haven't identified specifics, at best you'll spin your wheels and not accomplish much. At worst, you'll throw away a pile of money and get nothing out of it.

Identify the Message

What's the message you want your customers to associate with your business name or product? Keep it simple, descriptive of some benefit to your customers or problem solved, and differentiate your company from your competitors. Do you have a secret weapon? Do you have a product or service that nobody else has? If you do, great; use it to your advantage. If not, you need to keep your message focused on your customers, fulfilling their needs and solving their problems.

Identify the Budget

How much will you spend? Don't start asking that question when you get the bill from the advertising sales rep. Define the budget for marketing your product upfront when developing the plan and then manage to it.

How Will You Measure?

How will you measure and how will you define success? It's important to identify these issues before you begin. If you don't know what the end result should look like, how will you know if you got there or not? And, if you don't get what you hoped for, how will you change your plan to better achieve your goals?

You will need a way to test your results so that you can make improvements to the plan. If you're looking at a radio spot to promote a particular product or service, maybe you run two different spots to determine which wording and portrayal works best. Maybe two different print ads could be used to see which draws more calls from interested customers. Make sure to include a different website, phone number, email, or identifier so that you can tell which ad drove which result.

Some people will remember a radio spot from several years ago or confuse a competitor's ad with one from your business.

You must constantly monitor, measure, and test your promotional programs for effectiveness. If they aren't working, figure out why, and make the necessary changes. Don't launch a promotional campaign and then forget about it. The ad sales people love customers who do that. They can sell you spots without ever having to answer for the promotional effectiveness. That's the same as a big tattoo on your forehead that says, "SUCKER."

Action Plan

The action plan step is the tactical or implementation phase for putting your strategy into practice. The action plan phase of your plan could have dozens of different tactics for promoting and advertising your products or company. The specific tactics you choose will depend on your specific situation, budget, goals, and time frame. We'll cover some of the more common ways to promote your products. This is only a small list of possible implementation tactics.

The action plan phase of the marketing plan is really a two-step process. First, you identify the specific tactic you'll use, and then you create the action plan to make it happen. Let's first discuss the tactics and then how you go about creating an action plan to support the tactic.

Action Plan
    Advertising & Promotion
    PR Campaigns
    Networking
    Putting it to Work

This is an opportunity for you to be creative. There are as many tactics for promoting your business as there are people who can think of creative ways of promoting. From setting up a company Facebook page to advertising on paper tavern coasters, the whole world is open for your use. The key is getting your specific message to your specific customers. As long you keep that key principal in mind, the more creative your tactic, the better.

Advertising & Promotion

Typically, the difference between "advertising" and "promotion" is money. You have to pay for advertising, while promotion is free. The lines are fairly blurry when discussing some forms of advertising, so let's lump them together and call it all advertising. For a small business, you're always going to try to get the most bang for your buck. If you can get something for free or nearly free, then you'll do it. I don't think it's all that important to draw a distinction between paid advertising and free promotion. Let's just agree to call it all advertising and realize that some you'll have to pay for and some you won't.

Advertising for your small business can take many different forms, from television or radio spots to sponsoring the high school yearbook. Advertising can easily become a black hole where money goes and never returns. This is one area where having a well-defined budget and expectations are important. Know upfront how much you can spend in advertising and how you will measure your success. If your first attempt doesn't work, change your approach or change your form. Many advertising options for small business fall under the category of "donations" rather than advertising. Don't expect a high school yearbook ad to create new sales leads for you. However, advertising in a sports or arts program may lead to new customers. Which form of advertising you use will depend on your customer base and product line. It's usually a good idea to take small steps so that you can measure your success before spending big bucks on a full-blown campaign.

The whole idea in advertising is to get your message to your customers. You don't care to get your message to people or businesses that aren't target customers. Spending money to spread your message in the wrong place or to the wrong people is just wasting money.

Let's take a look at some examples of advertising.

Websites

Every business needs a website, period. If you have no intentions of using your site for the recruitment of customers, then you need it for general reference. In today's business environment, a business without a website is not viewed as a serious business. Even if your site is only serving as a business card with contact information and hours of operation, it's often the first impression you give to potential customers. Websites are easy to create and cheap. There's really no excuse for not having some kind of web presence.

When I consider doing business with a new company or a company that's new to me, the first thing I do is look at their website. If they don't have one, or it's really crummy, I try to find an alternative company with which to do business. And while that sentiment is not true for every consumer, you really can't afford to turn away any likely consumers.

Marketing Collateral

From business cards to brochures, product data sheets to samples, marketing collateral should define your brand and your products. Most small business owners can't afford fancy Fifth Avenue created marketing material. Consider how you can stretch your budget to get the best material available. Even if you don't have much of a budget, don't put out crummy material. Some items can be printed or even copied in black and white on a copier. A product data sheet or Material Safety Data Sheet (MSDS) probably doesn't need to be a four-color print job. If you have to choose between good design and good color/materials/printing, choose good design.

A well designed marketing piece can be used for many years. As your budget increases, you can change the printing or medium to spruce up the piece. However, a cheap design will look cheap no matter how fancy the printing or paper.

If you can only afford to produce one good piece of marketing collateral, make it your business card. You'll hand out your business card several hundred times a year. In many cases, your business card will be the only piece of collateral that a prospective customer will see. Spend the extra money to get your card designed by a professional so that you can always put your best foot forward with every contact.

Direct Marketing

Direct marketing can include such approaches as direct mail, email, phone solicitation, and lead generation. If you are using purchased mailing or calling lists, it's important to first define the type of lead for which you are looking. Most list agencies will be able to sort out their database into subgroups that meet your criteria. If you're selling industrial supplies and equipment, it doesn't do any good to solicit families. If you're selling cosmetics, you're probably wasting your time soliciting sporting venues. The more clearly you can define your customer, the better your list agency will be able to define the list you purchase.

Depending on your business and market, direct mail may be an excellent choice for contacting customers and generating leads. This is where getting a good list is really important.

Define your customer and purchase a list that is as close to it as possible.

Social Media

Social media has become a popular promotional tactic in the past couple of years. It's based on the premise that by building personal relationships with people, they will be more likely to buy your products when they need them or recommend your company to a friend who is in need of products like you sell. It can be a bit of a challenge to justify this activity in terms of time and costs, because it seems to be a large black hole where you pour your time. However, the costs associated with social networking activities are low in terms of hard dollars spent. It's really a question of your time.

There are dozens of different social networking sites, and different brands pop up every day. As of the writing of this book, the following social networking sites were fairly effective for mainstream work.

Twitter: This micro blogging site enables users to send "tweets," messages of 140 characters or less. It's an excellent tool for communicating with customers and presenting your brand. The search engines apparently give tweets favorable recognition, and heavy keyword use can bring traffic to your site.

Facebook: This is a social networking site where users can add and communicate with friends, send messages, and build an elaborate profile complete with pictures, video, and games.

Facebook has recently added the ability to create business pages, an area which is growing rapidly. The complete extent of the benefit is yet unknown, as this media is in the infancy stage. I expect it will continue to grow and become one of the most favored venues for businesses, even more important than a company web page in the future. Facebook is excellent for engaging people who like your company or for promoting your brand.

LinkedIn: This is a social networking site for business professionals. It's essentially an elaborate professional resume. The service is an excellent means of branding for a professional, but it does less than most other sites at communicating to a particular group and generating traffic.

YouTube: This is a video sharing website where users can upload and share videos. YouTube has seen phenomenal growth in recent years and is one of the best social networking sites for corporate branding, communication with customers, and promoting your corporate website.

Please recognize that by the time I finish typing this page, the social media players will have changed. These are just a few of the more important players in the social media market as of mid-2011. This is a fast moving medium and one that takes a considerable time investment. However, the payoff is huge traffic, brand awareness, and customer communication.

Newspaper

Most newspapers have several opportunities for paid advertising and free promotion in the course of a weekly news cycle. Paid advertising is the most obvious method. As with any paid advertising, you want to make sure the paper's readership demographic matches your target customer. Many newspapers today have a print version of the paper and an on-line version of the "paper." Check the demographics of each and determine if either version is a good match to your target customer demographic.

In addition to buying an actual ad, you can also use some of the free or nearly free options available in the paper. Most papers have a section that runs weekly in the Sunday paper that lists newsmakers in business. This is an opportunity to highlight new employees, promotions of existing employees, or awards or significant accomplishments of you or your employees. The calendar of events is an opportunity for you to list open houses, facility tours, and speaking events that you or your employees are leading.

Radio & TV Advertising

Radio and TV advertising can be very effective for your business, if the venue and time slot deliver the appropriate demographic. Business owners have to be very careful that their target customer is actually represented in the stations' demographic. Frank discussions with the advertising rep for the station about your intentions and targets will be helpful. If the rep can't deliver the demographic you need, go elsewhere.

Don't get suckered into trying a program if the audience isn't right.

Industry Advertising

Most industries have professional journals and magazines that cover the news and newsmakers in that industry. This can be a good venue for advertising, again, if the demographic fits your needs. The benefit of industry publications is that the target audience tends to be focused in a particular area.

Guerilla Tactics

Most business people are familiar with J. Conrad Levinson's 1983 best seller, Guerilla Marketing. The book identifies tactics for small businesses that are free or nearly free and highly effective for certain businesses. While I'm not saying you need to go out and buy the latest version of the book, I am suggesting that you think about nontraditional methods of reaching your customers.

Public Relations

While public relations has a different meaning in a large corporate setting, the small business can use many free methods to get their word out. It is in this context that I refer to public relations for small business. Some examples are:

Press Releases

One of best tools in the small business owner's public relations toolbox is the press release. A well written press release is bound to get some mention in the local business section of the newspaper. In the best possible scenario, this might lead to an article or television interview. News outlets are constantly looking for interesting news and public interest stories. While they have lots of national and state stories they can carry, they'd much rather tell a local story. You just need to give them a compelling reason to do so.

When writing a press release, follow the standard industry format. If you don't know how to write a press release, then do a little research so that you can utilize the proper format and tell a newsworthy story. If your press release is seen as an advertisement, it likely won't get mentioned. The local media want to help; you just have to do your part.

By becoming an industry resource to the business editor or one of the reporters that covers your industry, you stand a greater chance of getting your news release turned into a story in the paper or on the TV news. When you see interesting or important news articles or industry papers about your markets, share that information with the reporter or editor. By being helpful and not self-serving with your industry information, you're more likely to be seen as a credible news source when it comes time to get your story covered.

Website Blogs

Write a blog for your business. Attach the blog or link to it from your website. Anyone can write and manage a blog. It's not about writing a novel. In fact, short to the point stories are the norm. If you're going to write consistently long articles, then they must be entertaining and/or informative. People aren't going to read a three page article that drones on about nothing.

Your blog entries can be a combination of information about your business, your industry, special events at your company, interesting stories about your employees, and even special sales. It can't be a constant sales pitch, however. If it is, no one will come back.

Charity & Civic Volunteer

Become a volunteer with a local charity or civic group. Pick a group that you have interest in and get to work. A leadership role with a well-known or respected civic or charitable group will give you, your employees, and your company credibility, not to mention add to the good work that the group is doing in your community. I've never seen a company that adopted a "give back" attitude get anything but a positive response from their good work in the community.

If you have expertise in particular areas of business or your industry, offer to teach classes in those areas to local entrepreneurs. Local business incubators and small business development centers are always looking for volunteers to help mentor entrepreneurs and lead training classes. This can be a good way of gaining credibility within the business community and among the public. By associating yourself with worthwhile organizations that help others learn what you've already learned, you are seen as an expert in your field.

Speaker & Workshop Leader

In addition to speaking and mentoring in a business incubator setting, you can offer classes on your own and give talks. Find a local restaurant, hotel, or business services company to donate space in return for bringing in customers. You can give a free or paid talk or conduct a workshop on a topic that your customer base will hopefully find interesting. By giving the talk or conducting the workshop, you gain credibility as an expert in your field.

Most civic groups that meet regularly, like Rotary, need speakers to entertain and inform their membership. Depending on the size of your community, there will be from three to dozens of these type groups that are regularly seeking speakers.

Networking

Networking is a free or low-cost promotion strategy that puts you in front of customers, competitors, other local business owners, and employees and individuals who can help promote your business by word of mouth. While there are many organized networking events through business groups or civic clubs, it can also take place in a casual and opportunistic way.

If you are a member of local business groups such as the chamber of commerce or a BNI group, don't attempt to meet as many people as possible and hand out all your business cards. The idea with networking is to make deep connections with a few selected individuals and bring value to the relationship. That is, find out about the other individuals' businesses and find ways to make connections, introductions, or referrals for them.

Don't try to make a sale in the first five minutes of talking. In fact, don't try to make a sale at all. Successful networking is about giving, not getting. If you give on your side of the relationship, the other side will do the same. You will build a valuable business relationship and over time have a network of people promoting your business for you.

Networking is a long-term process. It will not always generate immediate results. While you may get lucky, plan on developing a network of business partners and friends who support one another, direct leads to one another, and serve as resources to support one another's businesses.

The Elevator Pitch

"So, what do you do?" How do you answer this question? It's called the elevator pitch, and it may be the most important 10–30 seconds of your business life. Whether at a cocktail party, convention, business meeting, or chance meeting, you are frequently asked what you do and have only a short window to engage your target with a compelling and interesting response that will make them ask more questions about your business.

An elevator pitch is a brief statement about who you are, what your business does, and why anyone should care. The emphasis should be on why anyone should care. Here's the idea: You're in an elevator with a potential business investor or customer, and they ask what you do. You have about 30 seconds, or the length of the elevator ride, to tell them about your business and get them intrigued enough to keep talking to you when you reach the lobby.

Write out your elevator pitch and practice saying it in a relaxed and confident tone. Only you know your business and the different aspects of your work. You will need different elevator pitches for different situations and audiences. The only way to get good at this is to script the pitch and practice delivering it. Often you'll find that in saying out loud what you have written, it doesn't really work. Don't just read your script in your mind, say it out loud, and practice in front of people who can give you constructive criticism.

What should you include in your elevator pitch? Here are a few thoughts to help you craft your ideal message:

How are you unique? – Why is your business or service any different than that of your competitors?

Speak to your customer's pain - Nobody cares that you have a specialty food shop. But if you have a food store that specializes in fully prepared meals ready to eat for working parents with families, now that might be really helpful and convenient for working parents.

Make it interesting – An excellent elevator pitch should get you pumped up. If you're flat and lifeless, why would your prospect care what you're saying? If you have a great story or passion, work that into your pitch.

Keep it simple – You can't make a single story work for every situation and every prospect. You need to build an arsenal of components that you know backwards and forwards that can be woven together for just the right message for each audience. Write down each message variation and rewrite them until they are perfect. Then practice, practice, practice.

It's not about you – In case you missed that point already, it's about your customers and how you can make their life better. Your customers don't care about you. They care only about themselves. If you can keep that point in mind, you'll have a better chance of developing an interesting elevator pitch.

Putting it to Work – The Action Plan

Putting these various tactics into practice is the key to the marketing plan. If you don't actually do something, nothing will happen, and all that time spent researching and planning will be wasted. Develop a system for managing your marketing tactics that works for you and your company, or use the simple system that I've developed for small business owners to manage the process.

I like to use a simple spreadsheet to identify the various tactics that a business is using, when the particular tactic will take place during the year, which employee will be responsible, and how much the budget will be for that tactic. This gives you an overall look at your particular tactics and when they are slated to run. You can define the time frame as cells in the spreadsheet that correspond to a month or week within the year. Assign a color to the cell when the tactic is supposed to run. You can assign meanings to different colors that represent when deadlines occur for a particular event, like a magazine ad, or special promotion effort in the newspaper or radio. The spreadsheet is your visualization of the entire process.

On a separate spreadsheet, identify each tactic and list the individual actions that are required for successful implementation. Again, use the individual spreadsheet cells to identify time frames. You are essentially creating a little Gant chart of the individual activities involved in the tactic. Let's look at an example tactic and some of the individual activities that might be involved.

Tactic: Advertisement in Seasonal Special Section for Newspaper

Our example company is a residential pool supply and service company that will be advertising in the spring homeowners special in the community newspaper.

Individual activities required: Identify the specific activities involved in the successful completion of this tactic, which employees are involved and responsible for each activity, and the budget associated with each. Confirm the critical path(s) and back-date each activity so that it can be started in time to meet the individual deadlines.

Identify the specific goal of the advertisement: We want to push our pool opening service complete with water testing and chemicals. In previous years, we have sold approximately 50 pool openings each spring. There are over 400 pools in our community, and we want to increase our market share of openings to 25%, or 100 pool openings per year. Typically, when we open a pool, the customer will also purchase their chemical supplies as well as water testing and other maintenance supplies from that company. They also tend to buy activity accessories such as floats from the company that opens the pool.

Identify newspaper deadlines: Discuss physical ad requirements and time deadlines with a newspaper representative. All other activities related to producing the ad will be scheduled based on the deadline. All physical activities related to the business will be back-dated based on the run date of the special section. These two dates are what's known as the critical path. All activities related to each of these dates will be scheduled based on having the action completed before the deadline.

Create special pricing: The sales group will work with the accounting department to identify the specific services and products involved in the special and the likely add-on sales to a create price that will be interesting to our customers, but still allows us to make a profit.

Create the ad: Work with the creative department or an outside marketing group to create an appropriate ad for the tactic goals and identify time requirements of the newspaper.

Confirm labor requirements: If we increase our opening from 50 to 100, we will likely need additional technicians to complete this work. We will discuss the labor requirements with the operations manager to identify his labor needs for this increase in activity.

Hire additional technicians: Give new labor requirements to the human resource department or outside staffing company to bring in new employees in time to get them trained for the new business activity.

Train technicians: Train the new technicians in our methods and procedures for opening a pool as well as cross selling activities to meet our sales goals.

Monitor

Not to be forgotten is the last step, monitoring. It is just as important as the other steps, but frequently never happens. You've researched and planned and devised and scheduled and now you're tired and just want to get to work. Your tactic takes place and you start thinking about the next one without analyzing and documenting the results of the former tactic. Did you compare the actual results to your goal? If you don't monitor your activities, you'll never know whether they are working and whether to do more or do less of that particular activity.

A critical component of the monitoring is figuring out upfront how you will measure success of each tactic. That should be a component of devising the goal. Make each goal specific and measurable. To suggest that you want to increase sales from a particular line of product advertising is entirely too vague. We want to increase sales by 3.5% in the residential line of vacuum cleaners or as in our example, we want to increase sales of pool openings by 50.

Once you have a specific and measurable goal, decide how you will actually measure. In most cases this will be obvious and clear. But if you have two or more activities working at the same time, you need to spend a little time devising a way to tell from where the potential increase in business is coming. How will you know if new business is coming from a social media campaign or that newspaper ad you bought? Use special departments, phone numbers, and web splash pages to identify and segregate traffic and purchases so you have a method to measure the increased activity and identify from where it came.

As you get data from each tactic, compare what you did and how you did it to the results you got. Consider changing the copy, color, pricing, or layout to get different results. As you tweak your tactics, note the change in performance and try to continually improve your results. When you hit on a great tactic, try to use it as a template for future tactics.

Summary

Creating a marketing plan can be a simple exercise if you follow the plan. Do your research to understand your industry, market segments, competition, and customers. With a critical eye, review your own company's pros and cons. Plan your strategy by identifying your unique sales proposition, brand, product pricing, distribution channels, and promotional goals. Create action plans to put your tactics to work. Finally, measure the results of your marketing activities, and make corrective action to improve your results.

See our other small business advisory books at Amazon or www.BusinessStartup101.com.

Business Start-up 101: From Great Idea to Profit…Quick!

Business Plan Template: How to Write a Business Plan

About the Authors

Chris Gattis

Chris started what is now Blue Point Strategies, LLC, a business consultancy, in 1984. He works with business owners who are struggling with the business part of running a business. From start-ups to turnarounds, Chris works with owners of small businesses to develop strategies and systems so they can achieve the financial success that drove them into business in the first place. Blue Point Strategies offers workshops, classes, consulting, and one-on-one coaching to assist business owners in achieving their dreams.

Chris has a background in corporate finance and operations, having served in various direct capacities, including CFO of the nation's largest privately-held insulation and construction products distributor; credit manager for the U.S. division of a multinational construction products manufacturer; and director of a small plastics manufacturing business. He has over 27 years of successful experience managing start-ups and turnarounds of large and small businesses as well as financial analysis, budget formulation, strategic planning, team building, and risk management. Chris has managed small businesses, wrestled with unreasonable demands from banks, and struggled with cash flow to make payroll. He understands the needs of and demands on small business owners.

His consulting experiences range from advising individual clients on real estate financing and development activities to managing start-ups and turnarounds of small businesses. He also has advised on site selection and expansion activities for a major Japanese automaker and various Tier 1 auto suppliers.

Chris has served on local planning and zoning commissions and development authorities, giving him keen insight into dealing with local cities and towns to further his clients' needs. In addition to his consulting practice, Chris serves as a business coach for local entrepreneurial development centers, an instructor for an area technical college, and a keynote speaker.

Blue Point Strategies, LLC
Huntsville, Alabama
www.BluePointStrategies.com
cgattis@BluePointStrategies.com

Felica Sparks

Felica Sparks of Ad4! Group, has been a small business advocate since she was 8 years old. It was the desire to be responsible for her own allowance that inspired her to start her first business, a local lemonade stand. From that lemonade stand, to becoming a state vice president for Future Business Leaders of America as a junior in high school, Felica has always had the entrepreneurial spirit.

Felica's adult career started out in the financial arena, working in small local and regional banks in the Huntsville, Alabama area. Working for the smaller banks gave her the freedom to be more of a hands-on partner with her commercial clients. It was from the desire to be a part of the commercial client's business growth that sparked the desire to become even more integrated in commercial development.

After 13 years in the financial industry, Felica joined one of her commercial clients and went into advertising and marketing at one of the larger Huntsville firms. Several years later, Felica got the entrepreneurial bug again and started the Ad4! Group. Since 2005 she has been concentrating on brand development and marketing strategies.

Ad4! Group
Huntsville, Alabama
www.ad4group.com
Felica@ad4group.com

www.BusinessStartup101.com

17916218R00049

Made in the USA
Lexington, KY
04 October 2012